WINSTON
the TRAVELING DOG'S
Christmas

by
Cynthia Anne
Finefrock

Faithful Friends Publishing
ISBN 978-1-7369459-6-4 (hardcover)
ISBN 978-1-7369459-7-1 (paperback)
Vectors by Adobe Stock
First Edition

CynthiaAnne.com

This book belongs to

_____

and is a gift from

_____

FELIZ
NAUGHTY
DOG

It was the first week of December, and Winston was busy ripping apart the tissues from the tissue box. Mid rip, Winston's mom called his name and asked if he wanted to read Christmas books before bed.

Several of the books mentioned a "Naughty or Nice List." Apparently, if you're on the Naughty List, Santa Paws doesn't bring you presents on Christmas Eve!

"Oh no," thought Winston. "I just assumed my cute face guaranteed presents! I better do a bunch of nice things before Christmas Eve so Santa puts me back on the Nice List."

The next morning, Winston got straight to work.
He went to a coffee shop called StarPups
and got a puppermint mocha for his mom.

He was really proud of himself
for not licking the foam off of it.
This was something he normally did.

After his morning coffee run, it was time to go shopping for gifts. Cheese and squeaky toys make great gifts, right?

When he arrived home, he carefully wrapped the presents with special wrapping paper.

He then strung the lights, decorated the tree, and baked Christmas cookies. What a busy day!

Winston was feeling great! It felt so good to do nice things for his family and friends. He decided to throw a howliday pawty to celebrate the season.

There was dancing, decorating gingerbread houses, and even a chance to dress in silly Christmas costumes!

"Eat, Drink, and be Hairy!" Winston barked with glee.

At the end of the night, as his guests started leaving, Winston was eyeing the cookies he had baked for Santa. Surely his mom wouldn't mind if he ate just ONE cookie...

Well, one cookie turned into TWO, and two turned into THREE. After eating all of that sugar, Winston was full of energy. He knew he shouldn't run in the house, but he couldn't help himself! He took one zoom too close to the Christmas tree and CRASH! An ornament fell to the ground and broke into pieces.
Oh no...

Winston was used to leaving accidents in the house, but nothing like this. He felt awful about breaking the ornament! He had been such a good boy lately, and now he had messed up all of the good progress he had made. That's when his last remaining guest (and also one of his wisest friends) reminded him that it's okay to make mistakes, as long as you learn from them. "I will do better tomorrow!" Winston vowed.

FROM: Winston

MERRY Christmas

So the next day, Winston put his mistake behind him and decided it would be a fun idea to write a letter to Santa Paws. This year, he really wanted a new dog bed and some chew toys. Paws crossed!

DEAR SaNTA!

After much anticipation, and lots of good deeds on Winston's part, the big night had FINALLY arrived. It was Christmas Eve!

Winston watched Christmas movies and sang Christmas carols ("O Christmas Treat O Christmas Treat" was his favorite), then left cookies and carrots by the fireplace for Santa and his reindeer.

Afterwards, he put on his pajamas and snuggled in for a long winter's nap.

When Winston awoke the next morning, he was not disappointed. Sitting next to the Christmas tree was the new dog bed he asked for, and there was an even bigger surprise in his stocking. It was a plane ticket for his next big adventure! Thanks, Santa!

After a morning of exchanging gifts with his family, Winston had one last gift he had to give...HIMSELF!

The past few weeks taught Winston the importance of being a good boy all year long, not just around Christmas. He also learned that giving is more fun than receiving!

BUT... if the foam on his mom's coffee went missing only a couple of times throughout the year, Winston figured that wouldn't be enough to land him on the Naughty List. Nobody's pawfect, right?!

Please don't forget to leave a review for the
Winston the Traveling Dog series on Amazon or Goodreads.
Winston loves reading them and your support is greatly appreciated!

Stay connected

Website
CynthiaAnne.com

Instagram
@WinstonTravels_

Facebook
@WinstontheTravelingDog

After authoring three books in the *Winston the Traveling Dog* series, author and photographer Cynthia Anne Finefrock felt compelled to add to the series with a book that captures the holiday spirit. What started in 2021 as "25 Days of Winston" on Instagram — a Christmas-themed Winston post for every day in December leading up to Christmas — has turned into a yearly tradition and inspired *Winston's Christmas.*

Beyond her excitement for spreading holiday cheer, Cynthia is passionate about experiencing as much of the world as possible through the lens of her camera. It was this passion that began a comical text exchange of Winston edited into remote destinations, which eventually transpired into the award-winning *Winston the Traveling Dog* book series.

Cynthia has degrees from the University of Southern California and Cornell University. She is a certified physician assistant and currently lives with her furry roommates in Scottsdale, Arizona, USA.

Made in the USA
Las Vegas, NV
19 March 2025

19831928R00017